TO;

God loves you!

Elma P Lomack

A Foolish Woman,
But God!

Evangelist Elma P. Lomack

Kingdom Builders Publications LLC

© 2020 Elma P. Lomack
A Foolish Woman, But God!
Kingdom Builders Publications, LLC

All scripture quotations, unless otherwise indicated, are taken from the Holy Bible, King James Version (KJV), Public Domain.

ISBN:
978-0-578-76201-2

Library of Congress Control Number
2020921827

Printed in the USA

Authored by
Elma P. Lomack

Editors
Wanda Brown
Lakisha S. Forrester
Kingdom Builders Publications

Cover Design
LoMar Designs

Cover Photo
ID 177485885 © David Herraez | Dreamstime.com

Contents

———————⟩⟨⟩⟨———————

Introduction

I thought about writing a book about my life for several years but didn't start finally writing until late 2017. I went through lots of situations and had my share of ups and downs with things to figure out and tough decisions to make. Some were good decisions, and some weren't. I know I'm not the only one who has made bad choices in life.

I almost gave up and wanted to end it all because of decisions I made. But I am glad I made the right decision to hang in there.

I was once a foolish woman in love with my man, falling in love with the looks and likes of him without the investigation of his character.

I poured my heart out in this book. As you read this memoir, please have an open mind. You may experience multiple emotions through these pages. You could conclude I *was* foolish, or you could have empathy and pity for me and cry your eyes out as you read this book, but for certain, everything I went through was all a part of God's plan. I had to go through some things to get the anointing God had for me.

Maybe you can relate to some things I went through. Maybe you can't. Either way, we all get vulnerable and can put ourselves in bad situations. Perhaps you will realize sometimes it is easy to get into things, but it is even harder to get out of them.

Life is not easy, but you can make it with the help of God. You don't have to give up. As long as the Lord is on your side, you can go through anything if you just trust Him. You can't depend on man, nor can you trust man more than God. Man will let you down and put you down, but God will pick you up. I just didn't realize it until later on in life. God was with me the whole time.

Many days I cried, sang songs to myself, and praised God a lot. Every chance I got, I prayed and asked God for help. I could not have made it without the Lord and prayer. Nobody can do you like the Lord can. My God is an awesome God.

It is my hope you will be determined not to be foolish. Whatever you are going through, God is there with you. I pray you will understand God will look out for you and take care of you no matter what. He wants what's best for you and He will deliver you from all foolishness. He loves you even if you don't love Him like you should.

Speak positive words over your life and draw closer to God. Take God at His Word, then others will look at your life too and say, "Wow, what a life. What a strong woman. But God saw her through."

SCRIPTURE

*I will bless the Lord at all times: his praise
shall continually be in my mouth.*

Psalm 34:1

Chapter 1

In the Beginning

Growing up, I did not know what it felt like to have a family with a mom and dad in the home. I was five years old when my dad died and was the youngest of nine children. My mother was a churchgoing woman. She took us to church every Sunday.

Mother, my sister, brother, and I moved from South Carolina to Connecticut when I was going to the fifth grade. There were two brothers already living in Connecticut. One of my older brothers wanted us to come to the beautiful state. Initially, he had a two-story house for all of us to live in. Later, he bought a three-story house for us.

When in high school, I wanted a boyfriend. The problem was, not too many boys talked to me the way I wanted them to talk to me. Although I wanted the attention of a boyfriend, I was reserved and timid, so I kept to myself.

I knew girls at my school, but I didn't have

anyone to confide in. I had no one really to talk to except my mother. What teenager wants to confide in their mother? Of course I loved my mom, and I was her baby. I went places with her but was lonely without a dad to talk to. I was no longer my dad's little girl, and sorely missed not having him around. I looked for someone to love me and have fun with.

One day, while walking home from school, I decided to go a different way than usual. Taking the long way to my house, I spotted some guys standing on a porch. This one guy said something to me, so I paused my walk to converse with him. He was quite the looker, so I felt good having this moment in my day. We talked briefly, then we exchanged names — his name was Jamey. We talked about exchanging numbers. He didn't ask my age and I didn't consider asking his. I just gave him my phone number as he requested. This was my first step to becoming foolish.

Some days later, Jamey called and asked if he could come over for a visit. I was only 16, but without the consent from anyone, I excitedly said yes. I found out Jamey was considerably older than me. I didn't know at the time how much older. He told me he was 18 and I believed what he said but discovered later he lied to me. He was four years older.

Jamey lived on the street behind our house, but I did not know it. He picked me out because, according to him, he would see me outside in the back yard, claiming to himself he was going to have me one day. Initially, he showed his kind and nice side. I judged him mostly on his good looks, not by his character or his ways. What a foolish young girl I was, but God was looking down on me.

I fell in love with him because he showed me some attention. Other boys at school didn't seem to notice me. My dreams had come true. I was doing well because I finally had a boyfriend. I had someone to talk with, hang out with, and do things with. Jamey did not like doing things I enjoyed, though. I wanted to socialize by going to parties, taking walks in the park, and go to an occasional movie. He wasn't remotely interested in any of those things.

Because of his age, he seemed more like a

dad than a boyfriend. When going out on a date with him, it never seemed like a good date.

He lied all the time about many different things. When realizing he was an alcoholic, I should have left then and never looked back. I should have known he was not the one when he came to my house drunk. I had on rose-colored shades when it came to him. Love covers a multitude of sins, but never was there such a misuse of this saying. Being in love with him caused me to close my eyes and overlook his faults. I overlooked everything. In my insecurity, I held on to him because I thought he was the boyfriend I had hoped for.

Love makes one do foolish things. I thought he loved me. It's not that he didn't love me, I did not know what love was. I was so captivated by his sweet talk and charm. It's funny how guys can make things sound good and tell you all the things you want to hear. They will lie in a minute if it will benefit them. I was foolish and fell for it all.

As fate would have it, I got pregnant with Jamey's child. My older sister was pregnant too.

We did not want to tell our mom we were both
pregnant, but the inevitability happened. We had
to tell her. In response, she was hurt and
disappointed. I did not want to see my boyfriend
anymore because I was pregnant and only 16.
That made me mad. Mom advised me to tell him
I was having his baby because it was his baby too.
I told him about the baby and kept seeing him.

My mother found a school for pregnant girls
to go to until the baby was born. When I returned
to high school, no one knew I had a baby. I had a
beautiful baby girl at 17. I had my baby girl one
month, and my sister had her baby boy the next
month. Our babies grew up like brother and sister
together in the same house for a while. It was not
easy taking care of a baby and going to high school.

My mother died a month or two after I turned
18. She nor my dad got to see me graduate. I was
happy I accomplished getting my diploma.
However, I was sad at the same time.

I was thankful to finish school even though I
had a baby. I now had somebody perfect and
precious to love, and that love was returned. Now,

it was just my sister, our two kids, and me. I continued seeing my boyfriend because he was a part of my family. Our little girl, Darci, would cry every time he came around. That was another sign he was not the one for me, but I did not pay attention to that sign either. I was still young and foolish, but God!

In a few short years, I got pregnant again with another beautiful girl, Tisha. I was 19 with two kids. My sister decided to move to Washington, DC, with her son. After that, it was just my girls and me living on the second floor of our three-story family home. On the first floor was my older brother and his family, and on the third was my youngest brother.

I allowed my boyfriend to stay overnight one or two nights per week, and eventually he moved in. That's what happens when you let a man stay one night, then he wants to stay another night. Before you know it, he will move in and you'll be wondering what happened. Once he moved in, it was hard to get him out. I did not like the idea but wasn't fond of the idea of living by myself with two kids. He was always going out, staying out late, drinking, and gambling. I talked to him about it, but he would not listen. He felt like he was a man, and he could do what he wanted to do.

I was so foolish for keeping him in my life. My sister knew better. She left town to get a new start without her baby's daddy. I stayed with mine through all the ups and downs. We were a family...my own little family.

We bought a car which was always on the side of the road broken down. We later got a nicer car, and I was especially fond of it. One night, Jamey seemed to be itching to go out. He just had to go out. Wouldn't you know it, he called to tell me he had an accident with my car! I was sad he wrecked the car, but glad he was alright. The accident was down the street from the house. When I saw our nice car all messed up and completely totaled, I wanted to cry.

Jamey had a habit of coming home and finding something to argue about. He loved arguing about anything. He could switch to anger in no time flat. I loved him because I thought he was all I had. It is not good when you want to be loved so badly until you just settle for anything. I wasn't willing to escape my mental entrapment. I could have done so much better than him. I was a foolish young woman who longed for her dad. I wanted my boyfriend to take care of us, but he did not know how. It was all about him. It was what *he* wanted.

I was on my own with no mom or dad. I had to grow up and take care of my girls. I did the best I could. I did not know much about life or how life was supposed to be. I did not know God, but I still went to church. I loved going to church. I started going to a Skill Center, a training school, where I learned skills for a trade. After I finished, I got a job in the local unemployment office as a secretary. I liked the job, and I got along well with my boss and co-workers.

At home, I lived in silent frustration because of Jamey and our relationship. We had money problems. He would not help pay bills. I received assistance to pay rent from welfare and received food stamps for a while. Jamey could not keep a job because he ran the streets. He tore up the cars we had, and he refused to listen to me. It was not easy with two kids. I tried not to worry my brothers and sisters. I did not want them to know how foolish I was.

One day, I got tired of Jamey's mess and the way we were living and came up with a plan to leave him. I was working and the girls were in daycare. One of my older sisters who lived in New Jersey let the girls and me come live with her for a while after asking. I did not tell anyone else but her what my plans were. I gave my job a two weeks' notice, then I quit, packed my bags, and hid the bags so Jamey could not see them and connect the dots.

When you're going to do something, you need to have a plan and figure out how you are going to see it through. I waited until he went to look for a job. Then I got my bags, the girls, and called a cab to take us to the bus station. I left him five dollars, but I hid it so he would have to find it. Even though I left him, he was still in my head!

Chapter 2

Moved Out, But Not Moved On

I made it to my sister's house. She had a
husband and three boys. She was going through
issues with her husband, but I did not realize it at
the time. The plan was to stay with her until I got
my own place, but I just did not want to impose on
her and her family too long.

After a while, I decided I wanted my last
paycheck so I could have a little more money. I
made the mistake of going back to Connecticut to
pick it up. I was not thinking I might see Jamey
when I went back. Well, I ran into him and what a
surprise. He had been looking all over for me.
He was asking my brothers and sisters if they knew
where I was. No one could tell him anything. He
talked to me making all these promises.

He told me he loved me and wanted us to be
together. I went back to New Jersey, and the next

thing I know, he was at my sister's door. I could not believe he found us. He talked me into going back with him. I still wanted us to be a family and be happy. Love had me blind. I believed everything he said. I wanted so much for our relationship to work out.

What a foolish woman I was to believe him again! In spite of myself, I thank God for being with me. If only I knew Jesus as a personal Savior back then. I went back to Connecticut for a little while. He told me we were moving to his hometown in North Carolina. "Okay, this is an improvement. He's taking responsibility. This feels good," I thought to myself. I packed up all our suitcases and was ready to move, but he was not ready to go yet. Why was he dragging his feet on his own suggestion to move to his hometown? He was taking too long to leave town, so I told him I was going to my oldest sister's house in New York; and when he gets ready to go, he could come get us.

He was good-looking and he just swept me off my feet. I trusted him when he told me my mother told him to take care of me. I just wanted to have a two-parent household for my girls, which is something I did not have growing up. I longed for the luxury of a mom and dad in the house. That kind of thinking just messed up my life. That is why I needed God, but I did not understand it at the time.

With the tools you have, you must take care of yourself and your kids and not depend on a man to do that. A man will let you down and make your life miserable if he doesn't have a relationship with the Lord. You need to know the Lord and seek His guidance. I was lost and did not know it.

Chapter 3

New Place, New Family,
But Same Couple

When I got to my oldest sister's house in New York, the girls and I were only there for a little while before Jamey came to pick us up. I left a big trunk at the house already packed up with all my important things in it. I thought Jamey would have it sent to North Carolina before he left town. He said by the time he got ready to leave, someone had stolen the big trunk. I was upset and sad about not having my stuff. How foolish I was to trust him to take care of something that important to me. He was not a responsible person. It was not his stuff, so he did not care that it was all gone.

Finally, we left for North Carolina. We traveled on the bus to his hometown since we did not have a car to drive. All we had were some clothes and a little bit of money. There was a little excitement in me because I thought we were going to have a better life. However, Jamey did not tell me about the living conditions there. I didn't know anything about North Carolina or what we were going into. There was no information on how big the house was or how many people would be living in the house. I just thought the girls, he, and I would be together, and things would be alright.

We arrived to the bus station. His mother picked us up there. His parents lived in rural country. I did not know what the country was all about. It was a small town. I left my brothers in the city to come to a place I knew nothing about, just because I wanted to have my own little family.

My mother and dad were deceased, but I had my girls and my man. I nor Jamey were Christians yet. I had no one to teach me about how a family should be. Jamey was older so I leaned on him to help me take care of our girls.

I was still young and foolish, but God was there with me and I still did not have a clue. When the girls and I got to his parents' house and I saw how small it was, I was in shock. I was unhappy to be there. His parents, four brothers, a sister, two nephews, and one niece were living in the small house. I was in the country where I knew no one. I had no car and no family. What was I going to do? I felt stuck in a situation with no idea of how to get out.

I did not have much money so I could not go anywhere else. We had to stay in that small house with all those people. When it was time to go to the bathroom, there was none to go to. Everyone went outside to an outhouse. There was no running water except a pump. I could not believe it! I thought they were kidding when they told me I had to go outside. I was scared to go outside, especially at night. What have I done? I left the city for this life? I was so miserable. Jamey knew what the situation was, but I did not know what I was getting the girls and myself into.

That was not an easy life for a young girl with two daughters. I felt all alone with no one to help me or turn to for advice. I had to learn things on my own. I did the best I could with the mess I was in. I was not thinking right. How foolish I was for thinking things would be better and we would be alright. We may have moved to a new place, but we were still the same two people.

I hated when the weekend came. Jamey's dad would get drunk, come home, pick a fight with his wife, and then argue and fight with his sons. I could not believe he would do that every weekend. Jamey's sister moved out with her baby boy. Their family did not get along at all. If the dad wasn't fighting, the two brothers were fighting each other. I wanted to leave. If it were just me, it would have been much easier, but where was I going with two kids? My sisters and brothers had their own families and issues. I did not want to add to their problems.

Finally, we got a mobile home. I was so thankful, even though we put it behind his parents' house. Things got a little better because we had our own place. The trailer had a bathroom and running water in it. When we were at his parents' house, we had to carry water to the house to cook with and wash with.

I had another baby, and this time it was a boy. We were very happy to have a son, however, I felt trapped. Where could I go with three kids? I made my mental adjustment to live in the country. Jamey's mother took me wherever I had to go. I even started going to church with her. We got an old car, but it did not last long.

I wanted to get married. I did not think that through either. I was still living in a fantasy world.

23

I was thinking if we got married, I could get saved, give my life to the Lord, and then things would be better. I wanted to do the right thing and live right. God cannot work in sin or bless you if you're living in sin. I thought I could change Jamey. I was always fooling myself. You can only change yourself.

When Jamey agreed to marry me, I was happy about that. We were finally going to be a real family. After marriage, I changed the girls' last name from my maiden name to his last name. My son was the only one to have my husband's last name when he was born. It was good for all of us to have the same last name.

Later, I got saved and I thought things would get better. I did not know I would become the devil's target. My husband got a little better, but he was still drinking, smoking, and running the streets. He had a job, so I put up with it. I kept hoping things would change and get better. What a foolish woman I was, but God was there all the time. The next year, I got a job and was happy to have my own money. It was good we both had jobs and a car, but we could not save any money.

We struggled to keep bills paid and food on

the table. I believed God would make a way and take care of us. I joined his mother's church and started working in the church. No one tells you when you get saved and give your life to Jesus, life is not necessarily going to be easier. I just took for granted life was going to be better for me. I was still dreaming.

I made up my mind to go to Heaven and I wasn't going to let anything, or anyone stop me. I thank God I was saved. One afternoon when my mother-in-law, my girls, and I were at church, someone came and told me my mobile home was on fire. That was so scary because my husband and my son were at home. We could not get home fast enough. When we got there, the trailer had already burned down.

My husband was gone when we got there. Someone told us that he was in the trailer taking a bath. He left the bathroom door open so he could hear our son, who was asleep in the living room. When he saw smoke coming down the hall, he jumped out of the tub to find our son. He found him and took him out of the trailer. Jamey did not have any clothes on, but he did not care. He just wanted to get our son to safety.

I thank God that they got out safely, but his brother told him to go back into the trailer to save some clothes. Foolishly, he did. He saved the dress I got married in and two suit coats. He had to jump out the window. When he did that, he cut his arms pretty badly and a friend had to take him to the hospital.

Our son was traumatized to tears. He was two years old and did not understand entirely what was going on. He had no shoes on. He loved his shoes, and he wanted them. That was a sad and trying time. We had just bought some things to go on vacation to the beach that next weekend. Now everything had burnt up. The girls were crying because all their stuff was gone. We only had the clothes that we were wearing. I could not believe this was happening to us.

We had to move back in with his parents and that's not what we expected. Thank God our stay there was not too long. We bought a house in the city limits. We were happy to have a house and a pretty good car of our own. Since we were doing okay, I felt God was blessing us. We both had jobs, a new house, and the girls were in school now. I still hung in there and kept praying to God and believing things were going to get better. The

Lord had taken me through all of that and I was grateful. I was still a foolish woman, but God was there with my family and me.

Chapter 4

Going Through the Fire,
God Is Still With Me

It seems I was always praying and crying. I went to church to praise God and cry tears of joy. I loved going to church. I went all the time. When something was going on at church, or if someone I knew was having something at their church, I could hardly wait to get there. I grew so much by going and visiting other churches. It gave me a relief, and a sense of peace and joy. I had a hunger and thirst for God. I spent time with Him, sang songs to Him, and praised Him with all my might. I could not have made it through without God and the church.

My hope was in the Lord to save my husband. It seemed the more I prayed and cried out to the Lord for his salvation, the worse he got. I just prayed and prayed for God to deliver us.

Jamey started taking money from the house. Whenever he gave me money, he would come back later and demand it back. I gave it to him so I could keep peace in my home. I hid money in the most inconspicuous place — a set of Bibles on the shelf. I could not believe he found the money every time. It was like he smelled the money. The bills went lacking, but I never had anything cut off because I always paid a little something on them.

I was going through the fire, but I believed God would bring me out. I didn't know when, but I was just waiting for Him to do it. I was always praying for God to help me and strengthen me.

I became president of the young adult choir. At the time, I was the only one saved on the choir. I cried a lot at home and on the way home from choir rehearsal. My husband mentioned I was always crying, but he just didn't understand what I was feeling or dealing with.

I talked to God about the choir. I asked the Lord to send me some saved members for the choir. Then, saved people came. However, those saved people gave me problems just as much. Being from Connecticut, and being apart of a family church in North Carolina, I felt like an outsider. This could be why the choir members did not want to listen to me at times. I thought things would be better with saved people. It was rough being the president of the choir and a choir director. They would not pay attention when I directed the songs at times. I felt powerless in my marriage and in the choir. I lead songs sometimes but was very nervous to the point of shaking while holding the microphone. I loved to sing this one song entitled "Stretch Out." As much as I loved this song, my memory would escape me, and I would forget the words. I did improve over time because the more I sang in front of people, the better I got.

The children were getting older and I was feeling alone. I had one friend who was great at listening, but because she was single, she didn't have any good advice for me. Thank God I had the Lord to talk to and lean on. He was my strong tower. I could call on Him anytime.

Finally, I realized my husband was not going to change. I did not know what I was doing wrong. I loved him and I just wanted to keep my family together. Maybe it was all in God's plan for me to

go through what I went through in order to get me
to where I was going. God was preparing me for
something He had for me to do, so I had to go
through the fire. God wanted me to come out like
pure gold. I still did not know God was there all
the time. So many times, He felt so far away. I
asked the Lord, "Lord, how long do I have to go
through this?" It was a hard time for me, but I
knew God.

My husband picked up a new habit along with
smoking and drinking. That new habit was called
cocaine. He would not stay home with the
children and me, like we wanted him to. He came
and went as he pleased. I was clueless of where he
was or what he was doing. I hated his drug binges
because he was a different man. He was like a Dr.
Jekyll and Mr. Hyde. He was mean and would say
all kinds of negative things to me. He was only
thinking of himself. Jamey could stay out for days
at a time. We only had one car and he had it, so it
was hard to go anywhere that I needed to go.

He cheated on me with other women, but he
was not going to leave me for another woman. He
always told me he loved me, but I needed more

than his words. They were just not enough. It was not the kind of love I needed from him. I believe we were similar in that neither of us knew what true love looked or felt like. I don't think he had a good childhood.

Women were bold back then. They would call your house and think nothing of it. Whenever women called the house, Jamey would leave and come back early in the morning. Sex might have been another addiction he dealt with. He loved sex and he wanted it and had to have it no matter what. He did not care how I felt about it.

I lived in silent frustrations in my home and at my church. Work was an outlet for me. I was good at my job and that made me feel good. I had friends to hang out with on the job. We shared things, we laughed, talked, prayed together, and some of us would have lunch. We had a lot of fun together. We were like a family. I hated when it was time to clock out. I was forced to face my sad reality. Home. That was the place I loved the least and I would rather stay at work than go home.

Thank God He kept me in my right mind.

He took me through it all and I praise Him for giving me strength. I read scriptures that helped me, like **1 Corinthians 10:13**:

> *There hath no temptation taken you but such as is common to man: but God is faithful, who will not suffer you to be tempted above that ye are able; but will with the temptation also make a way to escape, that ye may be able to bear it.*

God was always faithful to His Word. When my oldest daughter, Darci, decided to go off to college for four years, my husband was happy about that. He wanted all his children to go to college or the military to make something of themselves. Even though he did not go to college, he encouraged others to be better for themselves.

All wasn't bad with Jamey and me. We had some good days in our marriage. I tried focusing on the good days. I liked when we did things together or just sat around the house talking and laughing.

He was still drinking, smoking a lot, cheating,

33

and doing cocaine. He went to prison twice, but Jesus kept me both times. Each time he stayed about three or four months. The children and I were glad to have some peace around the house. I would go visit him on the weekends.

When my husband was in prison, I stopped taking birth control. There was no need to take it. The last time he came home, it was a surprise to the children and me. We were not informed of his release. Needless to say, I got pregnant with a fourth child. I had difficulty raising the three we already had; essentially, there was no bliss for me. Our youngest was 12 at the time, so I thought I was done with having babies. Here is another example of me as a young and foolish woman, but God was there all the time.

Embarrassment hovered over me due to having a baby at 36 years old. It was hard to tell people. I became so depressed trying to hold that inside. I slipped away to another church for solace and prayer. I needed the Lord to help me deal with being pregnant and telling people. After being prayed for, I felt better and began telling people the news. We already had two girls. I

wanted to have another boy so badly and it was all
I thought about.

When I told the children I was having a baby,
they could hardly believe it and thought I was
playing, but of course I was for real. My pregnancy
was a struggle. I thank God for helping me to get
through it. At the time of delivery, I was in labor
all night, so the doctor assisted me and delivered
our newborn daughter the next morning.

I was asleep when I had all of my children. I
did not know what it was to have natural births. I
did feel labor pains. I could not have made it
through without the help of my sister-in-law and
God. She was there with the 1st birth. With the 2nd
birth, I was alone and fell asleep during delivery.
The 3rd child, when my water broke, I fell asleep
before I ever got in the delivery room. When I
awoke, I looked at my stomach, and he was out!

I wanted to have two girls and two boys, but
Heaven sent another girl. My best friend came to
stay with me for support and help take care of the
baby. At first, I was not excited or happy about
having another girl. It took me a few days to come

35

to grips with having my third girl. After a while, I became attached to her and dressed her up every day. I was thankful she was healthy. I brought her home on my birthday; I had just turned 37. I started seeing my children as blessings. **Psalm 127:3** says:

> *Lo, children are an heritage of the LORD: and the fruit of the womb is his reward.*

Darci was in college in Charlotte, North Carolina, when my baby was born. Darci came home to meet her baby sister. My two oldest girls and niece named the baby. They named her Jayla. In wanting a boy more than anything, I prepared myself to name my son; except that was not in the plan. What you want may not be what God wants for you. Only God knows what is going to happen in your life. I am glad I read **Isaiah 55:8**:

> *For my thoughts are not your thoughts, neither are your ways my ways, saith the LORD.*

It is good to know God's ways and thoughts are better than ours. Sometimes we think we know what's best for us, but only God is qualified to know what is best for us. How foolish I was to think I was an expert of knowing what's best for my children and me! I thought having a family and holding on to a man who was inevitably not good for me was the best choice for me. Nevertheless, God saw me through it all, the good and the bad. I am so grateful He did.

There are now four children to fend for. I did not have the greatest examples to follow but I did what I thought was best for them. I learned how to cook and be a mother. The children loved my cooking because that was all they knew. They didn't have any grandparents to go visit and cook for them.

Darci would take her baby sister to college with her periodically. People thought Jayla was her baby and I, the grandmother. I felt some kind of way, but I refused to let it get me down. I knew who she was, so it didn't matter. Darci graduated from college and had a son. After a while, she came back home to live. She brought her boyfriend with her but didn't stick around because of my husband's dislike for him. Her choice for a man looked familiar through my own lens. He was not for my daughter and we wanted better for her. She went to work and my second oldest daughter, Tisha, got herself a mobile home. She also had a son. Darci moved in with her sister. Tisha had a nice jeep; she was doing well for herself.

The girls met men and started dating. They were nice men who had jobs and cars. Darci met a soldier and they moved to California. Tisha got married. She had a beautiful wedding. Her father walked her down the aisle. That was a special, touching moment to see them come down the aisle together. It was a happy day. Her sister was in the wedding. She also helped with the wedding. Our son Larry was in the wedding, and my baby girl Jayla was the flower girl. Our grandsons were in the wedding also, as ring bearers. That was a good time for us. It was a family affair — a day to remember. The wedding was elaborate but not costly, thank God! The wedding was followed by a reception at the church.

Jamey remained true to his addictions and I was still having difficulty at the church. I felt I was in a hole and could not get out. I tried to do what the Word of God says, especially after I read **James 1:22**:

> *But be ye doers of the word, and*
> *not hearers only, deceiving your*
> *own selves.*

My husband was still taking the money out the house and the bills kept getting behind. I could not pay the bills like I wanted to, and I had too much pride to ask anyone in my family for help. With the knowledge I had, I did the best I could.

I made sure I paid my tithes and a dollar offering. I believed if I paid those, God would take care of us. In **Malachi 3:10**, it says:

> *Bring ye all the tithes into the*
> *storehouse, that there may be meat in*
> *mine house, and prove me now*
> *herewith, saith the LORD of hosts, if I*
> *will not open you the windows of*
> *heaven, and pour you out a blessing,*
> *that there shall not be room enough to*
> *receive it.*

I believed paying my tithes and offerings made
a difference. At first, I paid my tithes out of my
net pay and did it for a long time. I was doing well
until one day I heard a pastor say tithes should be
given on the gross pay. He said you should be
giving God your best, so I gave on the gross. I gave
my tithes and offerings no matter what was going
on in my life since 1979. I believed God would
take care of His own. If you honor Him, He will
honor you.

I kept believing God would open the windows
of Heaven and pour out a blessing for all that
concerned me. I wanted to obey God's Word. I
had to be a doer and not just a hearer. Living for
God and going to Heaven were important to me. I
could not let anyone stop me. At work, men tried
to talk to me, but I had to let them know where I
stood with the Lord.

Even though I wanted somebody to take me
away from all I was going through, I could not give
up on my goals of serving God and going to
Heaven. I might have been a foolish woman, but I
was wise enough to know I could not let my guard
down. I knew distance would save me from the

men on my job. I laughed and joked with them, but that's as far as it went.

I was foolish when it came to my spouse and believing in a fantasy world. I wanted my life to be like the folks I saw on TV — happy, loving, and fun. I saw how the husbands treated their wives and kids. I longed as I dreamed to have the perfect life like TV land, but TV land is not always based on reality. I had to realize TV did not show the ups and downs that real people go through.

Things may not always turn out the way you want them to be, but I believed the song that says, Jesus will work it out! I sang this song with my girls when they were younger. It was the song we sang mostly when we were guests for choir anniversaries when the choir could not attend. I truly believed He would work it out for us one day.

I praise God for the songs we sang on the choir. They all meant something to me, especially the song, "Lord, Help Me to Hold Out." I loved that song and asked Him to help me. Another song we sang was, "Oh Lord, I Want You to Help Me." Those songs helped me through what I was

41

going through. Being saved may not be easy, but God did not tell us it would be. I am really glad Jesus is on my side and I can talk to Him about anything at any time.

Singing with my girls was a happy time in my life. We stopped singing together once they got older, but it was fun while it lasted. You have to do things with your kids and have fun. We would all go to the park sometimes and then go out to eat. My husband would go to church with us periodically. Every time he went to church, he'd go up for prayer and get saved. Then he would come back to the seat and make the girls go up for prayer. It did not last long because within the week, he'd go back to doing what he used to do...back to drinking, smoking, and in the streets even more. His behavior made me often sing the song, "Nobody Knows the Trouble I've Seen."

Later on, my husband started having drug dealers come by the house. He brought an old van and put it in the back yard. He would go in the van and do his own thing. He did not have seats in the back. He used it as his man cave. He was always buying old cars which broke down on the way home from the used car dealerships. We were on the side of the road a lot in our lifetime. My husband always worked on the cars we had. I prayed for the cars to run okay. We bought so many used cars, a man from the church asked if we had a used car lot. Finally, my husband got tired of used, broken down cars. He heard a radio commercial about a car dealership giving people a second chance to buy a car. In 1997, we went to look for a new car, but did not find one we liked. Jamey told the car salesman I would come back the following day and look. "If she finds one, let her drive it home so I can look at it because I have to go to work," he said. My son and I went looking the next day.

I was talking to the salesman and my son walked around looking at cars. He found this white car the salesman was not aware he had. It was a new 1997 Kia Sephia, 4-door sedan. It was nice and we liked it. The salesman let me drive it home to show Jamey. We came back and bought the car. I loved that car. That was our first new car. That day, Jamey declared we would not be buying anymore old used cars. There is an old saying, "Good things come to those who wait." I agree because we definitely waited a long time before we bought a new car.

We had the car for over five years. I paid the car off, then my husband started driving it. A little while after it was paid for, it started acting up. The car did not look the same once he started driving it and it did not drive right anymore. I did not like him driving the car to places it should not be going to. He would take it to buy drugs, so I did not want the car anymore. He was riding whoever he wanted to ride in it. Well, I saw it as my car, but his name was on it too; he co-signed for the car.

One day, Jayla, Dan, our grandson, and I were in the kitchen talking when we heard some noises sounding a lot like gunshots. We did not know our house was a target. I told Jamey I was taking the children shopping. He was in bed half asleep. When we returned home, I saw a few holes in the garage. I considered the shooters might have come back to shoot up the garage because we left with the car. I couldn't believe it. The children and I went in the house and started looking by the window in the front room. I saw a couple of bullet holes in the wall and a bullet on the floor. By this

time, Jamey was awake and I told him what I saw.
He called the police, and they came out and
looked around. Jamey knew why it happened.
Later, he disclosed why. It was a drug deal gone
bad and they blamed him for it. I was so thankful
we did not get hurt and it never happened again. I
was a foolish woman, but God took care of us.

When I went to work and came back, there
would be men at the house. I was so fed up with
his mess and all the stuff he was doing, the
drinking, smoking, going out, cheating, and having
men over at the house all the time.

He did go to church sometimes when we had
revival but was not successful in maintaining a
relationship with God.

Loving to pray as I do, I went to my church
and prayed like never before. I cried unto the
Lord. I told God I could not take it anymore. I
wanted him to do something to my husband to get
him to come to his senses. I did not care what it
was as long as my children and I didn't get hurt. I
put my husband in God's hands. When I left
church, I had peace like the Bible speaks of in

John 14:27:

Peace I leave with you, my peace I give unto you: not as the world giveth, give I unto you. Let not your heart be troubled, neither let it be afraid.

That night, I was asleep, and my phone rang. The voice on the other end said my husband had been shot and was transported to the hospital. I went back to sleep. Someone knocked on the door and woke me up again. I went to the door and they told me my husband got shot and I should go to the hospital. I went back and got in the bed again. Then, the phone rang again. I felt like I was not going to get any rest that night. Finally, I got up and called Tisha to go to the hospital with me.

That was really early on a Saturday morning. When we got there, he was in surgery, so there was nothing we could do. I had to work that Saturday. I told my daughter to stay until her dad came out of surgery. I called my son and told him to go over after work to be with his sister. I went to work, and I told my co-workers what happened. They were surprised I would even be at work after my husband was shot.

It was better for me to go to work. I had to make money to take care of the bills. There was nothing I could do but wait at the hospital. My husband was in God's hands. When I got off work, I went home to change my clothes and freshen up. I called my daughter to see how things were. She went home, but my son stayed behind. She revealed that I might not want to go see him because he was plugged up to a lot of tubes and he looked pretty bad. She didn't think I needed to see him like that. I went up to the hospital anyway. I felt like it was my wifely duty to be there with him.

I prayed for strength and for God's help. I loved him; he was still my husband. I saw him and he looked bad, but God gave me strength. I went to see him every day when I left work. On the weekends, I stayed with him. He was in the hospital for a month.

One day, a woman and her mother came to

47

visit him. He was happy to see them. I waited outside the room until they left. My suspicious nature kicked in and I wondered if she was one of his other women. It hurt me a little to see them laughing and talking together. I asked him about these two women, and he told me they worked with him on his job. I felt like she was more than a co-worker. His face just lit up when he saw them, and they were glad to see him as well.

Suddenly, he got paranoid and did not want anybody coming in the room. The nurse wanted to know what was wrong with him. He was afraid that the men who messed him up would come back for him; but they did not come around him anymore. He was finally released from the hospital after a month, but he needed someone to take care of him at home for many more months. I did not like that. He had a tube for his liquid food to go in his body. I had to hang a new bag up when the old one ran out. He had another tube that went to a waste bag. I had to clean it when it needed to be cleaned. It was hard taking care of him, but by the help of the Lord, I did what I had to do.

I was a Christian and leaning on the Lord for

strength. It might sound crazy, but I was a foolish woman still trying to keep my family together, and honor my wedding vows, which was important to me. If only I had the mind to leave him. I was lost for ideas of what to do or where to go.

Back then, things were not like they are now. You did not hear about divorce or people leaving their husbands too much. Maybe I was afraid to leave because I had no one to help me. I felt all alone with my own family. I just believed I was stuck, so I accepted my plot in life and kept moving. I held onto the idea that one day the Lord was going to work things out for us.

I felt like I was in a hole. Every time I wanted to get out of the hole, it was like something was pulling me back down. I thank God there is help now for women who are going through any kind of abuse and want to get out of bad relationships. I wanted to leave, but I didn't have the confidence I could make it without a man. I prayed God would help me and show me what to do. I couldn't figure out what I was doing wrong.

If only I had a different mindset for my

children and me. I had pity for my children when they were younger. I hate thinking about what I gave up and what I put them through by staying with their dad all those years. I tried to be a good wife. I stayed with Jamey because I did not think I could find anyone else who would take care of us. I was damaged with low self-esteem.

I convinced myself I was not smart enough to leave and even worse, putting it on God that He wanted me to stay. Oh, how foolish I was. I thought I was doing the right thing at the time. I was a messed-up Christian. I loved God and His Word. I tried to live by His Word as much as I could. I did not realize I didn't have to settle for less. If only I had the faith and boldness to go out on my own. Despite my situation, God kept my mind. I also leaned on **1 Corinthians 7:13**:

> *And the woman which hath an husband that believeth not, and if he be pleased to dwell with her, let her not leave him.*

I thought I was doing the right thing by staying with my husband after reading that scripture. It is the choices we make in life that can mess us up for a long time. If we make bad choices, there will be bad consequences. When we make good choices, then we will have good rewards. We just need to make good choices in our lives and things will be better for us. I hate I made so many bad choices.

Mature folks always say, "If only I knew then, what I know now." I concur with that statement; however, we can't turn back the hands of time or go backwards. We just have to keep moving on by the help of our Lord and Savior. Without Him, we can't do anything anyway. I thank God for being with me from the beginning and He is still with me on this journey called life.

I am so glad for what Jesus said in **Hebrews 13:5**:

> *I will never leave thee, nor forsake thee.*

If we read the Bible and do what it says, we'll be better people and happier people. I am learning to take God at His word. It took me a long time to learn that. Sometimes I would say to myself, "Lord, I know you said you won't put more on me than I can bear." Things seemed so hard for me. I would cry unto the Lord.

My husband seemed to be getting better and started going to church. However, he was in and out of church and his behavior would get worse and I hated it. He did not understand what he was doing. He started doing the stuff he was doing before, taking off with the car at night, and hanging out in the streets. He wanted to do what he was big enough to do. He did not like being told what to do. He did not want to serve the Lord to the fullest. I would have dreams that he was doing drugs again.

Darci was living in Barstow, California. She got married, and Tisha moved to Atlanta, Georgia, with her family. Now, Larry, Jayla, and I were at the house with Jamey. Jayla was more like him, so they did not get along. They fussed a lot. He loved her and he wanted her to do something with her life. He was always on her about things.

Jayla loved to play all the time, but my husband did not play. She would play around with me. One day, she wanted to wrestle with me and try to throw me down on the floor. I prayed and asked the Lord to give me strength so she wouldn't get the best of me. I did not want her to think she could beat me. The Lord gave me strength to throw her down. I was so thankful for that and I felt pretty good about my win. Her dad told her to leave me alone, I was too old for her to be playing with me. We had some good times. It was not all downhill.

I was watching Joyce Myer on TV one day and she said to think on the good times we have, not the bad ones. I tried to do just that. Looking at preachers on TV helped me, especially when I was not going to church. You need to find whatever can help you get through the storms in your life. You don't have to sit around all the time and feel sorry for yourself. You can enjoy Jesus by singing songs, praying, praising, and reading the Bible. Around the house, I loved to sing songs like, "Come on In the Room," "Yes Lord," "The Lord Is My Light," and "There's A Storm Out on the Ocean."

My son moved out. He went to live with his sister in Atlanta. I turned his closet into a prayer closet. I put a light, blankets, and a pillow in there.

While I was in there, I spent time with the Lord. Every chance I had, I went into my prayer closet. I had church there. I'd often stay in there until I grew tired. It was my getaway. My baby girl was in school and I would let her stay overnight with her friends sometimes. I really would have the house to myself because my husband was in the streets.

In my prayer closet, I prayed for my husband, brothers, sisters, children, and grandchildren. I prayed for my friends and the neighbors. I prayed for the church, the pastors, and for the leaders in the White House. I prayed for the police, the sick, and the people in nursing homes. I prayed for everything and everybody, and I also prayed for myself. I prayed like the Bible instructs in **1 Thessalonians 5:17** and **Luke 18:1**:

> *Pray without ceasing.*
> *Men ought always to pray, and not*
> *to faint.*

I was serious about serving God, and I had a serious fascination for wearing earrings. I wore clip-ons because I didn't have pierced ears. The clip-ons would hurt my ears, but I wore them anyway. I stretched them out some in the back so they would not hurt so badly. I loved wearing them and wasn't totally dressed until I had on a pair. I would not go out the house until I put them on. I felt I needed them to look good. I didn't care if I was late to work or to any function. I just had to find the perfect pair of earrings to put on. Like a drug, I was hooked on earrings. Here I go again, a foolish woman...but God!

One night, I went to a church revival and I was praising the Lord. The Spirit told me to take the earrings off. When I heard it again, I took them off; I had to be obedient. I had it bad but did not know it. The Spirit broke the hold earrings had on me. I was now released and did not wear them after that night. I thank God for delivering me. I was free to praise the Lord more.

You can be addicted to anything, but God can deliver you from whatever it is. There is nothing too hard for God. I will let any unfruitful thing go because I want to live for God and give him my all.

I was on a mission to make it to Heaven and could not stop. I could not turn around but had to press on no matter how hard things were. I

wanted to get my crown and I could not let
anything, or anyone change my mind. My soul was
too important to me. When you live for Jesus, you
have to give Him your all. You have to be
committed and determined. That is what kept me
going and holding on. From the day I got saved, I
was serious about my walk with God.

One day, I felt like God was calling me to
preach the gospel. I did not want to preach. I just
did not think I could do that. I went to different
churches and someone would always speak
something prophetic to me. They would ask if I
was a preacher or minister. I told them no. They
would tell me they see me preaching or I was
supposed to be preaching. I kept denying it
because that was not what I wanted to do.
However, when God has something for you to do,
you have to do it sooner or later. I guess that is
why I went through so much at home and at the
church.

I had to be sure that God wanted me to
preach. I could not go by what people were
saying. I had to know, without a shadow of a
doubt, that God called me to preach. I had a

56

feeling, but I could not just go on that either.

I went to our church one day by myself and prayed. I cried out to the Lord. I could not leave until I had God's assurance He called me to preach the Gospel. I had to know I was called, and it was my time. While I was praying, the Holy Spirit told me if I opened my mouth, He would speak for me. He said, "Go and I will go with you." He put **Isaiah 61:1** in my spirit. It says:

> *The Spirit of the Lord*
> *GOD is upon me; because the*
> *LORD hath anointed me to preach*
> *good tidings unto the meek; he hath*
> *sent me to bind up the*
> *brokenhearted, to proclaim liberty*
> *to the captives, and the opening of*
> *the prison to them that are bound.*

When I left the church, I accepted the call, and I was ready to go forth with what God wanted me to do. I met with my pastor to tell him what God spoke to me. He did not believe me at first, and was not in favor of women preachers, but he knew I was determined. He could not stop what God said. He had me stand up in our quarterly

57

meeting and tell the church what God said to me. I set a date and a time for my first sermon.

If God called you to do something, don't let man stop you. You have to do what God tells you to do or you will not have any peace and you may be sorry you didn't obey.

I started preaching September 1999. Jamey wasn't where I was in the faith, but he stood with me and supported me. I thank God my husband did not try to stop me or hold me back. I preached at my church sometimes. I worked in the church with a smile and I always gave God the praise. I attended every church service and revival because I still needed to grow in the Lord. I kept praying for my husband, the choir, my children, the church, and myself. I read my Bible a lot. **Psalms 27:14** told me to:

> *Wait on the LORD: be of good courage, and he shall strengthen thine heart: wait, I say, on the LORD.*

The scriptures, singing on the choir, going to church, being a child of God, praying, and reading the Bible are the things which got me through tumultuous times. You have to find something that will help you make it through your storms. Sometimes you have to encourage yourself. You cannot depend on people to encourage you all the time; instead, meditate on God's Word, sing a song, and praise Him. That will bless you and lift your spirit.

I kept waiting on the Lord to bring about a change in my life. Even though my husband was still acting up and taking things from the house, selling, or pawning them, walking up and down the streets, looking bad, drinking, smoking, and doing drugs, I kept praying for him. Jamey was tall and skinny. He would get mad and curse me out. He was not big on talking positively.

He just took over our car. He would take me to work and be late picking me up. He was not working at this time so I don't know why he could not pick me up on time. Everybody would be gone before he came to pick me up. I would wait on him and sometimes I walked down the road, then I would see him coming. I was still a foolish woman, but God was there all the time taking me through and giving me strength.

Jamey had an anger problem. He would get mad quickly and fuss and cuss. He was always fussing about something. He'd fuss so much he made himself mad. I hated arguing with him because it did not do any good. I would just try to talk to him about something and we would end up fussing. I hated talking to him. I thought to myself, "Why do I talk to him? He is not listening. He is too busy fussing and getting mad." He would often leave the house, walking or he'd drive off with the car. I wanted him to leave so bad and not come back. I tried not to think evil thoughts, but sometimes I could not help it. He had a good side, and he had a bad side. I tried to focus on his good side.

We were like night and day. We did not like doing the same things. We looked at different things on TV. Sometimes he wanted me to watch what he was watching. He did not like sitting in chairs. He liked laying on the chair or across the bed to watch TV. I liked going places, whereas he liked staying at home. I wanted to watch romantic movies or shows that were funny, but he liked crime shows and movies with lots of violence. However, we both enjoyed eating sweets. I loved him and he loved me. We loved each other in our own little way. He always told me he loved me all the time, but I wanted him to show me instead of telling me. He was jealous and he didn't like for me to go anywhere by myself. It was so ironic for him not to want me to go places by myself unchaperoned, but he never wanted to go with me.

Jamey had a double standard. He would not allow me to talk and laugh with other men, but he could talk and laugh with other women. He was paranoid after he got shot and beaten with a baseball bat. He did not trust people. He slept with a hammer under the bed. There were times when he would not answer the door because he did not like people coming to the house.

I kept praying for a saved husband. I told the Lord that I did not want to die and not see my husband saved. My mother-in-law died before her husband got saved. After her death, her husband finally received Christ and started going to church about every Sunday.

61

The times my husband and I did go to church, we would come home fussing. I got to the point I did not want him to go to church with me. If we were going to be fussing all the way home from church, I would rather he stayed home. I did not have a lot of peace. Our children were not happy when they were growing up. They did not like seeing their dad act the way he did. They hated the way he spoke because he rarely had anything nice to say. One day, Jayla asked him why he was so negative all the time.

I did not curse, drink, or smoke; I was a church girl. I did not judge Jamey for what he was doing, but I did encourage him to do better. I don't think it was totally his fault; his parents were negative and fussed all the time as well. I often spoke to him about his bad behavior and habits, but he did not seem to care about anything I had to say. He was addicted to all he was doing. He could not stop on his own. He did not have the mind to quit by himself. When you want to stop something, you must have a made-up mind and the determination before it can happen. I wanted my husband to get some help, but he did not want any. He felt like he was okay just the way he was.

He did try to get help one time, but he did not want to give up his lifestyle.

Later, we bought another new car because the old car was messing up. However, we kept it; so we had two cars. We bought a 2002 Kia Spectra. That became my blessed car. I wanted to get a tag that said, "MY BLESSED CAR," but I didn't. We traveled a lot, visiting our older children in Atlanta.

My motto was: "If you can take it, you can make it." Like many others who have referenced this quote, I kept repeating it as I was going through my trials. We had some ups and downs, but we just did not have any real goals or ambitions to succeed in our lives. We were never taught about those things. It is good to have goals, so you'll have something to work towards.

Chapter 5

Peace Came Through
Testing Times

———————∂෩෩ᕲ෩———————

I worked hard on my job, at my church, and in my home. I tried to be the best I could be at whatever I did. One day, our children's choir leader took the children to Pizza Hut for the all-you-can-eat special. However, I ate too much pizza.

I went to the doctor for a check-up. The doctor said I had high blood pressure and gave me pills to take. They worked for a long time because they kept my blood pressure down. Then I started having more problems with my blood pressure. It was because I stopped taking the pills. I did not like taking the medicine. I made a decision to see if I could go without taking it for a while. It didn't work because my pressure went up again. I wound up at the doctor's office. I told him that I stopped taking the medicine. He was not happy. He told me I would be on the medication for the rest of my life, but I refused to accept that. I even stopped wearing my glasses to see if I could see without them. That did not work either.

The doctor put me back on the medicine. I went through a lot of different medications before he got one that controlled my blood pressure better. I was getting older, more tired, with mood swings and frustration on my job and at home. There was a lot of work to do on the job. We started working 12-hour shifts. We worked three days and were off four days for one week. Then the next week, we worked four days and were off three days. We had every other weekend off.

I did not go to church as much as I once did. I felt a little left out because I could not keep up with what was going on at church. Since I worked every other weekend, it did not feel the same when I did go to church. I started to get a little weak in my Christian walk. I did not pray or read the Bible as much as I used to, but I didn't turn my back on God or give up on Him. I still kept the faith.

People said I had changed, but I couldn't see

it. I was more vocal. I started speaking up for myself. I used to be quiet and let people walk all over me. In being nice to people, they took advantage of me. I just got tired of the way I was being treated, so I started telling people how I felt. They thought I was mean. My children thought the same.

I wanted to quit my job, but I couldn't because we needed two incomes. I didn't like going to work anymore. I hated the 12-hour shifts. At times, things got so hard I just wanted to give up. I was still a foolish woman in my mind, but God was there with me seeing me through. I kept praying for the Lord to help me.

One day, in 2005, I went to the doctor for my annual checkup. I had this young female doctor. She took the usual tests. When she came back with the results, she said I needed to have a hysterectomy. She acted as if I had to have it done immediately. I knew women who had the surgery done before me, so I thought I'd be alright. She said I could get the partial procedure or a total hysterectomy. I told my friends and family. My friends thought I should get a total hysterectomy,

66

but my family suggested I get a second opinion to be sure.

Jamey did not like that the doctor was a young woman. I decided to get a total hysterectomy instead of listening to my family for a second opinion. I did not have peace about the surgery, but I had it done anyway. I should have waited a little while before having it done; but once again, I thought I was doing the right thing.

The hysterectomy was done in May of the same year. I came out of the hospital after four days. I thought everything was fine. After a few days of being home, I noticed water running down my legs and it did not stop. It scared me, so I went to my surgeon. She examined me and when I got up, water started pouring out of me. She told my husband to go buy me some adult diapers. He brought them back to the office. I put them on, and the doctor told me to go to the hospital.

I went to the hospital and they kept me. The exams showed I had a hole in my bladder from the hysterectomy. I was taken back into surgery to correct the issue, but the doctor could not fix it.

For about two months, I was in and out the hospital. One time while in the hospital, the doctor put me in ICU for some reason. I don't remember why. While I was there, I kept pressing the button for pain medicine. I did not know the doctor changed my medicine; I had an allergic reaction. I felt so cold and I was trying to tell the doctor that something was going wrong, but she wouldn't listen. I could hear her calling my name as I was slipping away.

I thought I was dying, so I was saying goodbye and started prophesying to people, but nobody heard me. I was unconscious. When I finally woke up, I thought I had died and come back to life. The medicine made me really sick. When I woke up and was alert, I was by myself. I began pulling the intravenous tube out of my hand and pulled out the catheter. I didn't think I needed those things anymore.

I went to the restroom. When I got back in the bed, the doctor, nurse, security guard, and some others in white coats rushed into my room. They tied me down to the bed. I told them they did not need to do that; I would not get out of bed

68

again. The doctor gave me a shot and I was out.

When I woke up, the doctor had put the IV back in my arm and reinstalled the catheter. I was also given a blood transfusion. I stayed in the ICU for a few days and was then moved to a regular room. I was in the hospital for 14 days. Finally, I went home, just to turn around and go back to the hospital because the water began to leak again. When I got back, I was delusional, talking out of my head. I stayed in there for a few days before being released to go home again. They were unable to fix the leaking problem.

My sister from New Jersey came to visit me for a few days and I enjoyed her visit. However, her visit was cut short because she was not getting along with my husband. When she left, I felt so alone and abandoned. I started going downhill. My children came to visit me every chance they got. But for the most part, I felt like I had no one to help me or understand what I was going through.

I went back into the hospital again and the doctor decided to send me to Durham, North

Carolina, to a specialist because she had done all she could to help me. While I was in the hospital the last time, I started to think all kinds of bad things. I started hiding my pills when the nurse gave them to me. I pretended to take them, but I did not swallow them. I started to think the doctor was trying to kill me. She thought I was crazy. She had doctors asking me all kinds of questions. She even mentioned putting me in a mental facility. I told her to go ahead, I did not care. I was out of it and did not know what I was saying. The devil had my mind.

I did not watch much TV, but when I did, the only shows I watched at that time were about violence and murder. I was depressed but I did not realize it. While I was in the hospital, I thought about suicide. I thought about jumping out of the car and running into the woods where no one could find me. I was mad that I had to walk around with a catheter. I wanted to punish people by killing myself. My mind was really messed up. I was still saved, but I was a foolish woman. However, during that time, I'd forgotten about God. I was sick in my body and in my mind.

Things were so bad one time, I thought I was possessed by a demon and needed someone to come and cast it out. My husband did not want people to see me that way. When I came home, I stayed in my bedroom. I did not want to eat, watch TV, or get out of bed. I didn't even want to pray. I lost weight and I was in bad shape. Jayla did not want to come in the room. She said it was too hard for her to see me in such a condition.

My husband did not know what to do for me. He would not stay home with me like I wanted him to. I was alone and the devil was working on my mind. When you get weak, the devil will come in and take over if you don't stop him. I was too depressed to know what was going on. My husband told me he was going to put me in a mental facility, but I did not care. The medicine I was taking was messing me up. I started thinking about suicide again.

One day, I put a plastic bag over my head and tried to suffocate myself. When the bag began to suffocate me, I snatched it off. The devil thought he had me, but God was still with me, even though I had slipped away from Him.

71

On another occasion, Satan told me to get in the bathtub and drown myself. He said nobody loved me and I'd be better off dead. I filled the tub with water and got in. I laid in the tub and slid down under the water. But when the water got into my nose and mouth, I frantically got out of the tub.

The devil wanted me to kill myself. He will always try to take us out if God has a mission for us. Satan does not want us to serve God and do mighty works for Him. He doesn't want us to know God gave us power over him (the enemy). We have to realize God has all power. God would not let me die. I thank Him for his mercy and grace. He kept me when I could not keep myself.

Finally, my husband could not take it anymore. He called Darci to come get me and take me to her house in Columbia. He said there was nothing he could do for me. My children did not know how sick I was, nobody really knew.

Darci spoke to her brother and her sister who were living in Georgia. She told them to come home with her to pick me up and take me back to her house. She was going to take care of me. I thank God for my children. When they got to my house, Larry asked Darci if she was sure she wanted to take me in the condition I was in. She told him yes. She said God would help her and give her the strength she needed to take care of me. I wanted my children to stay home with me, but they said they had to go back home, and they wanted me to go with them. I was a foolish woman, more foolish than sick. It was a troubling time for my family.

I was in a deep state of despair. Darci did some research and said I had all the signs of depression. I did not like having to walk around carrying a catheter bag and having to do that really messed me up. I was ashamed, upset, and wondering, "Why me?"

Finally, my son convinced me to leave with them. I did not want to leave my baby girl, because she was only 15. However, I had two friends who said they would look out for her. Leaving my daughter put even more strain on my fragile state of mind. As we were traveling back to Columbia, Darci said she wanted to stop in

Darlington, South Carolina, to see my oldest sister.
I did not want to stop anywhere. I just wanted to
go to her house and confine myself to a room.

We stopped at my sister's house anyway, but I
would not get out of the car. My sister and her
husband came to the car to see me. She gave us
some food to take with us. She did not know I was
that sick. After the short visit, we headed to
Columbia. When my children and I got to Darci's
house, I laid on the sofa and stayed there a while.
She had a big dog. I did not want to go to my
daughter's house because I was afraid the dog's
barking would get on my nerves, but God kept him
quiet for me, and I was grateful.

My daughter had a second floor in her house,
but I did not want to go upstairs. I wanted to stay
on the first floor and not have to walk up and
down the stairs because I had to walk with that
catheter bag. The catheter bag and the medicine I
was taking, got me thinking God was punishing me
for getting the hysterectomy, which made me even
more depressed. I could not accept the fact I was
going through all of these issues. I wouldn't eat
much because I really didn't have an appetite. I

lost even more weight. I went from a size 16 to a size 12. I only wore dresses, skirts, and tops. I did not wear pants.

All I wanted to do was lay around and sleep. I was feeling sorry for myself. I wanted to be in the dark a lot. I wanted the lights off, the TV off, and I wanted everything to be still and quiet. My daughter left gospel music playing when she went to work but I would turn it off when she left. Darci came home frequently to check on me. She took a leave of absence from her job to help me. When she went back to work, her mother-in-law came from Charleston, SC, to help take care of me. My other daughter, Tisha, in Atlanta, also came some weekends to help out.

My girls went shopping to buy clothes for me to wear. They bought me a throw blanket to put over my catheter bag so when I went to the doctor it would not be as noticeable. I was very sensitive about the bag, so I never wanted to leave the house. I did not want to go anywhere. It was the winter season so when people saw me with the blanket, they just assumed I was trying to stay warm. I stayed in a state of depression for about two months. I was going back and forth to the doctor. My doctor in North Carolina referred me to a doctor in Columbia so I could get my prescriptions refilled.

Darci didn't think I needed all the medicine the doctor had me taking, so she started taking me off little by little. When I ran out of medicine, she refused to get any refills.

Finally, I started feeling a little better after I stopped taking all of the medication. I even started watching TV. I saw a man on one show who didn't have hands or feet, yet he was not having a pity party. He'd figured out how to do things for himself despite his situation. I, on the other hand, was sitting around feeling sorry for myself, not wanting to do anything. His story inspired me. So that day I decided to get up and start doing something for myself and around the house. I was glad I saw that show on TV because that was a turning point for me.

Wayne, our son-in-law, was in the Army and was away on duty for a while. When he returned home, he observed how much his wife was accommodating to her mother. I didn't get the feeling he was being mean, but he did tell his wife I had to get off the sofa and move upstairs to the guest room. He said he was tired of seeing me use my daughter to cater to my every need. He said I had to start doing things for myself...and he was right.

I traveled to Durham to see a specialist about repairing the hole in my bladder. She examined me, evaluated my situation, and said I needed to wait a month before she could operate on me. She wanted my body to get stronger to endure the surgery.

I was trying to do more for myself. I started going up and down the stairs and taking baths in the tub. Tisha came down from Atlanta one weekend and wanted me to go to church with them. I had not been to church in about six months since I had my first operation. I was so scared until I started shaking. I told her I would go next Sunday. "No, Mom. I am not coming back down here next Sunday," she said. She wanted me to go with them that Sunday. They left me alone and started praying for me and praising

God. A few minutes later, I calmed down and a spirit of peace came over me. We got ready for church. I took the throw blanket with me to church to cover the catheter bag. It was a good service. I thank God for my girls. After that Sunday, I started going to church again. I started praying again and reading my Bible once again. I loved reading **Psalm 118:17**:

> *I shall not die, but live, and declare the works of the LORD.*

I repeated the scripture over and over again. I started going outside, looking up at the sky, and appreciating what God had created. The sky was so beautiful. From that day on, I never took God or my life for granted again. I thanked Him for life and for each day He allowed me to see. God was, and still is, so good to me.

I'd been a foolish woman so many times, but God was there every time. Nobody can do you like the Lord. That was a dark time in my life. There were people praying for me everywhere, in churches and on prayer lines. I could not have made it through without the Lord, my family, and the prayers of people. I thank God for the prayers of the saints.

Wayne finished his tour and was back home to stay, so I no longer had my daughter to myself. I went to stay with Tisha in Atlanta for a few weeks. While I was at her house, I fell down the stairs with the catheter bag in my hand. I was alright, thank God. The incident scared her and my grandson, though. Later, I went back to Darci's house in Columbia.

Three and a half months after arriving in Columbia, I went back to North Carolina to pick up Jayla. I brought her back with me. I could not bear being away from her any longer. I was so worried about her. I needed to have her with me. I am so thankful the Lord took care of my baby girl while we were apart. I registered her at one of the high schools near Darci's house. The transition was not smooth for her. She did not like the new school at all, and she missed her friends and teachers.

Finally, I was well enough to have the surgery to fix the puncture in my bladder. We went to

Durham and I stayed at the hospital overnight and came home later the next day. I still had to have the catheter for a couple more weeks. When I went back to the doctor, she removed it. The surgery was a success. Praise God I did not have to carry the catheter bag around anymore. God healed me. He took care of me through it all.

There was a song I loved to hear entitled, "I Almost Gave Up." This was my testimony. When I heard this song on the radio, it brought tears to my eyes. There were several times in my life I just wanted to give up. I could relate to the words of so many songs. Songs like, "Can't Nobody Do Me Like Jesus," "Somebody Prayed for Me," and "I'm Yours, Lord," helped me get through challenging times in my life.

I thank my Heavenly Father for all He has done for me. What the devil meant for my bad, God turned it around for my good. The devil tried to take me out. I would not wish what I went through on anyone. I thank God for never leaving me when I was in a dark place and when I did not want to hear about Him, pray, or read His Word. Even though I stayed away from Him, He never left me.

I was torn up from the floor up. I stayed with my daughter for five and a half months. I spoke with my husband and I told him I did not want to come back to the same old mess. I was really tired of that old life. He said things would be different and he wanted me to come home. He said he missed us.

Darci and the church I went to in North Carolina had a surprise welcome home dinner party for Jayla and me. Larry and his wife and Tisha and her boys came from Atlanta. My sister, her husband, and my father-in-law came to the celebration as well. It was a nice welcome dinner with family and friends. I thank God for my family. Family is everything. They have always been there for me. It is good to have a loving family.

I have peace from the sickness I went through. It was a trying time, but God was there all the time. I was grateful for the scripture, **Philippians 4:7**, that says:

And the peace of God, which passeth all

*understanding, shall keep your hearts
and minds through Christ Jesus.*

After a month, the doctor said I could go back
to work. The day I returned to work was the same
day I got laid off. Others had already been laid
off. It was only God's mercy I didn't get laid off
while I was on sick leave. Honestly, I was glad to
be laid off because I did not like working there
anymore. I wanted to quit a long time ago, but a
friend told me not to. I am so glad I did not quit.
When they laid me off, I got all of my money.
That was a blessing! God is a good God.

Chapter 6

My Prayers Answered,
My Husband Delivered

In 2007, the Lord delivered my husband from alcohol, smoking, drugs, running the streets, and cheating. He did it all at one time. My husband got tired of what he was doing, so he prayed, and God delivered him. God can do anything if you want Him to, and if you let Him. He was a different man. He started going to church with me and reading his Bible. He got saved for real this time. I was grateful to God for finally answering my prayers and my husband's prayers.

I was a minister, but I still sang with the choir. I was over the choir for 15 years. We merged the choirs together into one choir. We now had a mass choir I sang on and directed. After a while, I gave up being over the choir. It took time for me to give up directing. I enjoyed singing and directing, but I would also preach every chance I got.

Things were good. I enrolled in a community college. I thank the Lord for allowing me to go to college without having to pay for it. I got financial aid from the college. The next year, I applied for a scholarship. Each year I was in college, I received financial aid and a scholarship. God blessed me to have money in my pocket while furthering my education.

I enjoyed going to school, but I could not go to church as much as I wanted to. I had to do my homework and keep my grades up. Some things you enjoy have to be put on hold when you are in school. You have to be committed, dedicated, and willing to make sacrifices. If you want something bad enough, you will do all you can to make it happen.

I wanted to give up so many times, but I made up my mind I wanted to graduate and walk across the stage. I had a goal, and I had to see it through to the end. **Philippians 4:13** really helped me:

> *I can do all things through Christ which strengtheneth me.*

If you want to do something in life, always think on this scripture. You can do anything you put your mind to when you have the help of the Lord. I learned there is always a bright side somewhere.

It was hard going to school and dropping my baby girl off at her high school in the mornings. Some days I had to be at school before my daughter needed to be at school. My friend, who took her granddaughter to school, let Jayla be a car rider with them. When Jayla got in the 11th grade, I bought her a car to drive because I got tired of having to figure out how to get her to school every morning. I bought my other children cars when they were going to school because they did not want to ride the bus. I wanted to treat all of my children the same, so I had to buy Jayla a car also.

After getting her a car, I could go to my classes in peace. I could get to school on time, and I did not have to drive fast. The college I went to was about 45 minutes away. I was not crazy about the ride to school nor the hard classes. At the end, I was glad when I did not have to go every day. Each year, I had to report to the campus fewer days. During my last year, I only had to go twice a week.

I worked very hard to pass all of my classes. I was a good student. I made A's and B's. I enjoyed going to class and talking to the teachers. However, I did not like my online class; my grade could have been better. I am grateful the Lord gave me the strength to get through those years.

The first time I went to college, I earned an Associate's Degree in Business Administration of Science. It was hard work, but I did it with the help of my oldest daughter, my husband, and the Lord. My husband helped by giving me time to study. He was very supportive and worked hard to help me reach my goals. He was proud of me and I was proud of him for changing his life.

I went back to get another Associate's Degree in Office Administration. However, I did not complete my degree. I was afraid I would get sick again and not be able to keep my grades up. Because of my health, I made the decision not to return to school.

I'm glad Jamey became a new man. The

Bible says in **2 Corinthians 5:17**:

> *Therefore if any man be in*
> *Christ, he is a new creature: old*
> *things are passed away; behold, all*
> *things are become new.*

We still had our ups and downs. Marriage is work. Every marriage has its problems. But you have to be willing to work through the problems together and keep it moving. You have to be able to listen and come to an agreement. The two are no longer two but have become one. If you love each other, God will keep you together when you work at it and keep Him first.

Early on when my husband wanted to fuss, I'd get mad and fuss right back. Later, I decided somebody had to stop fussing. I started singing a song or speaking in tongues, trying to keep my cool. I refused to fuss with him any longer. It didn't make sense to keep going on and on. You don't get anywhere by doing that. Now I try to think before I speak because **James 4:7** says:

> *Submit yourselves therefore to God.*
> *Resist the devil, and he will flee*

87

from you.

I meditated on the Word of God a lot. The Word of the Lord will keep you if you believe and do what it says. My husband began to pray every morning when we got out of bed. Sometimes we even read the Bible together. I was glad he was delivered from all this worldly stuff. He didn't hang around the people he used to hang out with, and he did not walk the streets anymore. The only things he did not change were his attitude and his negative thinking. He would encourage other people more than he did his family.

Jamey loved to paint the exterior of our house; he was a good painter. He would change the color of the house all the time. One day, he painted the house many colors. I started describing it as the house of many colors whenever I told people how to get to our house. I was glad when he repainted it just two colors. Soon, he started painting other homes for a price. Sometimes he wanted me to be with him when he painted. I would take him some water and some food to eat.

Even when he used to work on our cars, he

wanted me outside with him. He always wanted me around when he was doing something. Sometimes I had to help him with the car repairs. We'd be outside until 2 or 3 a.m. working on the car. I would sit in the car until he wanted me to hold the flashlight. I was really glad when we bought new cars, because in the winter it was too cold outside to be working on them.

Every time I went somewhere without him, he would call me several times. If I did not answer the phone, he would get mad and leave messages. He wanted to make sure I was safe. He told me to make sure I locked my car doors when I was out. He wanted me to call him when I got to my destination, but I would sometimes forget. Besides, I didn't want to call him...EVERY TIME. Sometimes people would even ask why he called me so much. If I were at a friend's house and he would call, they would always say, "There goes your husband."

I felt like a slave. At the house, he wanted me to always do something for him. For instance, he would be laying in the bed or chair looking at TV. The remote would be in the room with him, but instead of getting up, he'd call me to come get the remote for him. Also, when I was home, he wanted to have sex. That was another reason I would leave and take my time coming back home.

He loved working outside in the yard. He kept our yard looking good. People always commented on our yard. The neighbors started working in their yards after they saw how nice our yard looked. Jamey planted flowers and dogwood trees. He wanted me to come outside and help him with the yard, but I wasn't an outside person. I loved the inside, cooking and cleaning up. I told him we needed to make a deal that he'd work on the outside and I would work on the inside.

One day, he started playing gospel music on the radio outside. At first, he would bring the tape player in the house at night. In the morning, he would put it back outside on the porch. Then he started leaving the tape player outside all night. He would play the music so loud. He said he wanted the neighborhood to hear the music. Sometimes preaching would be playing on the radio. He started leaving the radio on all day long, even when we weren't home. People liked listening to the music. No one complained about the music being too loud, and no one ever stole the radio from the yard. After a while, he put a big boom box on the porch which played even louder. He played the radio on the outside for years. God gave him favor in the neighborhood. God was with us. People gave him respect and they enjoyed talking to him. Everybody knew him in the neighborhood. He was not a stranger because he could talk to anybody. I called it his radio ministry. My husband was saved, and he wanted the people in our community to be saved.

We had drug addicts and alcoholics in our neighborhood, but my husband did not like them walking up and down the street, passing our house. He did not like people coming to the house. He preferred to go to the road or in the front yard to talk with them. He was a funny man. He could make you laugh with the things he said. He spoke his mind and he was a little jealous.

He started singing on the male chorus at church. He loved singing the songs, "Where the Thunder Don't Roar" and "People There's a Train Coming," on the choir. He could sing pretty

well. People at the church loved to hear him sing.
He used to clean up at church when they would
feed after service. He would also help clean up in
our house. He was particular about his clothes.
He had to look nice when he went out. He would
not go outside or anywhere without ironing his
clothes first. Even if he was going to sit outside or
cut grass, he had to iron his pants and shirt.

I may have been a foolish woman, but God
was there all the time. I thank God for the
strength to hold on and wait for Him to save my
husband. He may not come when you want Him,
but He will always see you through.

Chapter 7

God Will Take You Through Sickness After Sickness

———————— ༺༻ ————————

One day, my blood pressure went up as I was having pain in my stomach. I went to the emergency room to get checked out. They found out I had gallstones in my gallbladder. The doctor put me in the hospital and removed my gallbladder. He did not have to cut me like I thought. Instead, he put three incisions in my stomach with tubes in them. One tube sucked the gallbladder out and the other tube was to release gas. I don't remember what the third tube was for. I had a lot of pain before I had the surgery done in early 2012, but I felt better after it was over. The doctor gave me medication for the pain. This was a rough time for me.

I got sick again in the middle of the year. My blood pressure had gone up real high. I felt bad and was getting worse. I went to the emergency room and they sent me home. The next day, I went back to the emergency room because my blood pressure was still high, and they sent me back home again. I went to my family doctor and I started feeling worse in her office.

My husband and my sister-in-law were with me in the doctor's office. When the doctor spoke to me, I started talking out of my head. My husband got scared and started to cry, and that made my sister-in-law cry. My doctor called for an ambulance to take me to the hospital. In the ambulance, the paramedic gave me something to lower my blood pressure.

This time, the emergency room doctor had me take a blood test to see what was going on with me. He found out my sodium and potassium levels were very low. They kept me in the hospital for four days to get my blood pressure, sodium, and potassium under control. My children came to visit me. My son stayed with me the first night. The second night, Tisha stayed with me. I was glad they came to see me. I am so thankful I am still alive. Once again, God brought me through.

I may have been a foolish woman, but God

was there with me. I was able to go home the next day. I was feeling a lot better. I got sick because I stopped eating and cooking with salt. I knew I had high blood pressure, so I thought I was helping myself by not eating salt, but I was wrong. I did not realize I needed some iodized salt in my body. The doctor told me I could have had a seizure with my sodium and potassium being so low. I felt like I did have a seizure or something, based on the way I was acting in my doctor's office.

Later in the same year, 2012, I got sick again. My blood pressure was high again and I went back and forth to the emergency room. They kept sending me home each time. They were not checking my blood. My husband was tired from going back and forth to the hospital. Once arriving at the hospital, he was supposed to turn before he got all the way around the circle. However, he did not turn, but instead, he went around the circle two times. I said, "What's wrong? You were supposed to turn." I did not know what was going on with him. He finally told me he took some medicine before we left home.

I felt bad for going to the hospital so much. I

was scared because my blood pressure kept going up too high. I was hurting too. It seemed the more pain I was in, the higher my blood pressure increased. I tried to explain that to the doctors.

The next night, instead of going to the emergency room, I went to a clinic which stayed open until 10 p.m. They were about to release me to go home, but I was still feeling bad. The nurse decided to check my blood pressure one more time before letting me go. It had gone up again, so they called the ambulance to take me to the hospital.

The paramedics did the same thing as before. They gave me something to lower my blood pressure. Both times I went to the hospital by ambulance, my husband followed in our car. On the way there, I had to go to the bathroom, so the ambulance driver pulled over. My sister-in-law was with my husband in our car. They were wondering why the ambulance pulled over and stopped. Would you believe they pulled over and gave me the bed pan to use?

When I got to the emergency room, they

checked my blood and found my sodium was low again. I had to stay in the hospital until they got my numbers up. I was eating some salt but not enough. I was also drinking a lot of water. The doctor told me to slack up on the water. He said I was drinking too much water, plus I was on water pills. The doctor took me off of those pills because he said I was flushing the sodium out of my body. This time, my sodium was lower than my potassium. I stayed in the hospital three days, but when I went home, I felt better.

One night, I started to feel bad. My husband and I decided to go to another hospital, but I hate I did that. My stomach was hurting really bad. I stayed in the hospital three days and I felt sick the entire time. The doctor thought my heart was hurting, despite the fact I told him it was my stomach. He did not listen to me.

He wanted me to take a stress test to check my heart. The test came back fine, then he sent me home. I went home still feeling bad because he did not do anything for me. That Saturday night, I was in my bed and I really felt bad, but I did not say anything to my husband.

I felt like I was alone and was the only one going through. I did not think about someone else going through something worse than me. I could not go to sleep, so I started praying. I left the bed and laid down on the sofa in the living room. I rebuked the devil, and I gave him the Word of God. I told him I refuse to go back to the hospital again and he might as well loose me and let me go. I told the devil to get out of my body and leave. I told the enemy that I shall live and not die, and I was healed by Jesus's stripes. I kept praying because I had to take authority over my body. I told Satan to leave me alone, and I was going to go to sleep in Jesus's name. I felt a little better and finally I fell asleep.

Sunday morning, I realized God was with me all the time. My husband and I got dressed and went to church. A lady on the choir started to sing and I began to praise the Lord, and right then, the Spirit of God let me know I was healed.

I went home thanking God for my healing. God will do what He says He will do. I was going through sickness after sickness. The Lord was with me and took me through. What a mighty

God we serve! I realized God will do things in His time. You can't hurry Him; you just have to wait. **Isaiah 40:31** says:

> *But they that wait upon the*
> *LORD shall renew their strength;*
> *they shall mount up with wings as*
> *eagles; they shall run, and not be*
> *weary; and they shall walk, and*
> *not faint.*

I always believed things happened for a reason. I did not appreciate things like I should have. Through my sicknesses, I got peace and I realized God was with me. I became thankful and grateful for all things, the little and the big, and I appreciated life more. I was thankful to be feeling like myself again.

Many people take life for granted and at one time, I did too. I am so thankful for what I have learned from everything I went through. I am really thankful for peace of mind; there is nothing like it. I had to learn how to trust God. Nobody can do you like the Lord. Just like the scripture, **Psalms 34:8**, says:

*O taste and see that the
LORD is good: blessed is the
man that trusteth in him.*

Chapter 8

Dealing With a Sick Husband

One Sunday, my husband was singing on the male chorus and he looked funny. His mouth was a little white. When we got home, I checked his sugar. It was 560 mg/dl, and I told him he needed to go to the hospital. He said he drank too much sweet tea at church, but he would be alright. I called his sisters. They also tried to get him to go to the hospital. One of his sisters, who was a nurse, told him his sugar level was too high and to drink plenty of water and his numbers should come down. He decided to do what his sister suggested since he was not going to the hospital.

Later in the week, he finally went to the doctor to get his sugar checked. The doctor told him it was still over 200 mg/dl and that was still too high. She did further tests and discovered he was a diabetic. She wanted to put him on insulin, but he did not want to take the shots; he wanted pills instead. I was glad he got pills because I knew I would have to give him the shots. The family doctor told him to watch what he eats, not to eat so many sweets, and not to drink a lot of sodas.

He did not listen to the doctor. He ate a lot of sweets and drank a lot of sodas. He loved to eat candy, ice cream, cookies, and anything else sweet. He was also crazy about canned sodas. In fact, we kept them in the house all the time. Even I told him to stop eating so many sweets and drinking so many sodas. I think sweets and sodas took the place of drinking alcohol and smoking. Jamey did not eat enough vegetables, but he loved meat. He also liked his food fried all the time. He loved frying chicken, pork chops, and cooking pork & beans.

Jamey just didn't take care of himself. He was always cutting grass. He said cutting grass was his exercise. He'd cut our grass and then go cut other people's grass. He would not stop until he finished cutting all the grass in the neighborhood. He'd cut grass even when it was too hot outside. He sweated too much in the heat and would not drink enough water or cover his head. Once in a while, he would take a short break and drink some water or a soda. He just didn't listen. He did not want anyone telling him what to do. He had to do things his way. He said it was his life and he was going to live it his way, so I left him alone. I knew it was not going to do any good to keep preaching to him. I felt life was too short to be fussing over something which wasn't going to change.

One day, he got sick and we thought he had a bad cold. I brought him all kinds of cold medicine. He felt better after a while, but he still had a cough which wouldn't go away. I told him to go see a doctor, but he kept putting it off. In the middle of 2013, he went to a new clinic. The doctor examined him and ran tests. The tests showed he had a spot on his lungs. The doctor gave him some antibiotics to take and told him if he did not get any better he needed to go to the emergency room. It was Stage 4 lung cancer. That was a shock to us. Life was not the same for us after that. He went into the hospital before Thanksgiving and came out on Thanksgiving Day.

Jamey had to undergo more testing to see if the cancer had spread, and it did. It had spread to his brain and other parts of his chest. In 2014, Jamey started radiation to slow the spread of the cancer. After a while, his hair came out. That was hard because he loved his hair. He kept it dyed black all the time because he did not like to see any gray hair on his head or his mustache.

He did not want to go anywhere after his hair came out. He would only go to the doctor's office for his treatments. I bought him a toboggan to put on his head. After the radiation treatments were finished, the doctor started chemotherapy. He had to go to chemo for a while.

On Father's Day, two of our daughters took him to the family home. His dad had died before Father's Day. The family decided to have a cookout. His brothers were home from out of town. Darci and I were already over at the house because he was not ready when we left. As my two youngest daughters were bringing him on the drive over, he became sick and slumped over. They stopped in the driveway and got out and screamed that he was dead. Everybody started running to the car to see what was going on. That was a scary time for all of us. When we got to the car, we discovered he was passed out. A family member told everyone to move back to give him some air.

Someone called the ambulance, but they took too long to arrive. He finally came to and was confused as to what happened. The ambulance arrived and we told him to go to the hospital to get checked out. We wanted to make sure he was alright. We got to the hospital and the doctor said he was okay, but he wanted to keep him overnight for observation. Jamey refused to stay in the hospital because he wanted to go back to be with his family. We went back over to his father's house to the cookout and he enjoyed being with his family.

That night, he got sick again. I took him back to the hospital and they found he had fluid around his lungs. The doctor sent him to another hospital because they did not have the equipment to do surgery on him. At the other hospital, they drained the fluid from around his lungs and he felt better. Two days later, he was released.

He did well for a little while, but before long, I had to take him back to the hospital. The doctor said he had fluid around his lungs again. They drained the fluid out again. When he went back to the doctor for his chemo treatment, she told him she was going to put a catheter in his side so the fluid would drain at home.

He went for outpatient surgery to have the catheter put in. I did not like that because I knew one day I was going to have to drain the fluid. When we went back to the doctor, she told him there was nothing more she could do for him. She stopped chemotherapy and turned him over to hospice care. She said he had about six months to a year to live. He did well for a while. His hair grew back, and he started going to church again. My daughters took turns coming to help me take care of him. People prayed for him. My children and I were praying for him.

Taking care of Jamey was a hard job. I had to do everything from feeding him, giving him medicine, sticking his finger to monitor his blood sugar level, and giving him shots when his sugar got too high. I was not getting enough rest for myself and I was getting tired. Tisha took off work to help me take care of her dad. Darci came back and forth to help when she could, but she had her own family to take care of. It was hard for all of us. I could not get Jayla to help too much. She hated seeing her dad like that. She only went in his room when I asked her to help me with something.

One day, all the children came home, and it was good for us to be together again. I went to the bathroom and Jayla was in the living room. The three older children were in the kitchen talking. To our surprise, Jamey got out of bed by himself, walked into the living room, and fussed at Jayla. She got up and went in the kitchen.

He fussed at the children because they did not clean the house. I came out the bathroom and was wondering what was going on. I was shocked he had gotten up and walked. He had not walked by himself before that. I got him back into the bed so he would stop fussing at the children. They said they were happy to see his independence at first until he started fussing. The children felt it did not make any sense for him to get up just to fuss. They said he should have been thankful he was walking.

107

He apologized to the children for fussing at them. I would always apologize for him when he did something wrong. This time, he apologized to them himself, and that was good.

He seemed to be doing better for a few months. We thought things were going to be alright. He started going to church again because the girls brought him a hat to wear. We were enjoying being together as a family. Dan would come visit us too, and my husband enjoyed seeing him. Jamey also liked to read the Bible and pray.

One time, he made two of the other grandsons, who came to visit, read the 23rd Psalm. They were tired because they had just gotten home. They just wanted to go to sleep, but he kept them up. A few days later, our dog died, and my husband went out to bury him in the woods behind the house. My husband was sick, but the Lord gave him strength. He was a strong man and a fighter. He fought the sickness as much as he could. Our grandsons helped him drag the dog into the woods. The day our dog died was a sad day. God knew we could not take care of a dog and my husband.

Initially, hospice had a nurse come out three times a week. Afterwards, the certified nursing assistant (CNA) came to take care of him four days a week. They did not work on the weekends. I really appreciated their help. The CNA fed him, bathed him, and changed his sheets. The nurse checked his medical condition. At first, the nurse drained the fluid from his lungs. That was a big help to me. I was glad about it because I did not want to do that job. However, Jamey wanted me to learn how to do it in case his lungs needed to be drained when the nurses were not there. I learned to do it, but I wasn't happy about it.

My husband began to weaken so much so until he was unable to get out of bed or walk anymore. He had to stay in the bed all the time unless someone helped him get to the wheelchair.

Wayne came and helped for a few days. My husband liked having him around to help him. Larry came home to help me a few days as well. I really did not want Larry to come because I was afraid he might get hurt again. One time, he was trying to help his dad back into the wheelchair by himself and he complained of excruciating back pain. My sister-in-law would come over and bathe Jamey. She knew how to change the sheets with him in the bed. We had to change his pamper when he needed it changed on the weekend and at night. The CNA took care of those needs during the weekdays when she came to the house.

I would have the deacons take turns helping me get him out the bed to sit in the wheelchair and I called them back when he needed to get back in the bed. All the children had to go back home. Hospice had a chaplain come visit my husband once a week; Jamey enjoyed those visits. I also had a minister from our church to come help me sometimes. Even my pastor came over to help. When different people came over to help me, I could go shopping and do other things for an hour or two.

I was so thankful and glad for the help. I was able to get some rest when my children were there. I could not have made it without everyone helping. At one time, I was taking care of my husband day and night by myself. I may have been a foolish woman, but God was with me all the time. **Psalm 27:1** says:

*The LORD is my light and my
salvation; whom shall I fear? the
LORD is the strength of my life; of
whom shall I be afraid?*

I am so grateful the Lord gave me strength
when I needed it. You don't have to worry in life
because God will provide. He will watch over you
and take care of you. I had to look to Him.
Nobody can do you like the Lord can. If you just
lean on our Father, He will not let you fall.

When our two oldest daughters would come,
my husband would sometimes talk bad to them.
He fussed a lot at Tisha, probably because she
spent the most time with him. She took off from
her job to help me take care of him for a few
months. He would hurt her feelings, but she did
her best to help him. It was hard work taking care
of Jamey. It took a toll on all of us.

It got to the point where we had to watch him
because he would climb out of bed and fall. He
balled up his fist and tried to hit at me whenever I
got close to him. I coaxed him and told him,
"Come on!" Then I stood back so he would not

111

hit me.

When we left the room, he would put his legs over the bed rail. He climbed over the bed rail onto the floor and we helped him back to the bed. He tried to crawl out of the room one time, but he could not figure out how to get out the door. I was asleep. When I woke up, he was on the floor. I called for EMS to get him back into the bed. I hated calling them so much, but I had no choice. My daughter and I could not lift him off the floor. We couldn't manage his weight because he was taller and heavier. The first responders understood he was sick. They were kind about it. Sometimes EMS would show up and other times the police officers would.

I slept on the air mattress at night so I could keep an eye on him. Eventually, I had to put it beside his bed when no one was in the room so if he climbed out the bed, he would fall on the mattress.

He got to the point where he would not help us at all. He would not hold onto the bed rail when I tried to turn him over to clean him up and

112

change his pamper. It was hard for my daughter and me to change the sheets with him in the bed.

That was a tough time for us. My children came as often as they could. I was thankful they found out about the Megabus. Initially, they were able to travel home for one dollar. The fare later increased to three dollars, but it was still affordable. They were able to visit more often and help me with their dad. I know my husband was glad to have them home too. I read in **1 Thessalonians 5:18**, where it says:

> *In every thing give thanks: for this is the will of God in Christ Jesus concerning you.*

I am always giving thanks. I take nothing for granted. God is good no matter what we go through in life. We may not understand why we go through some of the things we encounter, but one day we will.

Jamey and I would read God's Word and I played CDs and the radio for him. Sometimes the church would give us a DVD of the Sunday service and he'd enjoy listening to that. He loved the **23rd**

Psalm and he always wanted me to read it to him. We loved the **first verse** that says:

> *The Lord is my shepherd; I shall not want.*

My daughters and I made sure he took all of his medicine on time. He also took a lot of Goody's Powder packets. We sometimes had to crush his pills and mix them in with the powder so he would take them without fussing.

Knowing Jesus as our Savior is the best thing for us. We don't know when it will be our turn to leave this world, but Jesus did promise us peace in **John 16:33**, which says:

> *These things I have spoken unto you, that in me ye might have peace. In the world ye shall have tribulation: but be of good cheer; I have overcome the world.*

I realized, through my husband's sickness, we can experience peace in our tribulations. Even though some days were hard when it came to taking care of him, my children and I always handled him with love. We treated him the way we would want others to treat us. I believed in honoring my vows and I vowed to be committed to my husband in sickness and in health, until death do us part.

So many people don't take their vows seriously, but I did. I took my vows before God and I could not break them because they meant something to me. I may not have been happy all the time, but he was my husband. Even during the times when he was in the streets and I did not like him too much, I remembered my vows. We loved each other in our own way, and it kept us together for 36 years.

Be encouraged to wait on God to send you a spouse, because you might choose the wrong one and have a lot of misery. If you would just be patient and wait on God, I promise you would be a lot better off. Don't be young and foolish. Do not make bad decisions, because they will lead to bad consequences. I did not realize that then. Make sure you know the Lord as your personal Savior. Let Him lead you in the right direction. Seek Him for the right mate before you fall in love with anyone. Love will make you foolish and blind. I fell in love at first sight. I fell for his looks and the attention he gave me. That was a bad decision on my part, but I did not know any better at the time.

Chapter 9

Time for My Husband to Leave This World

My husband started sweating one day and I called the nurse. I also called our pastor and a minister to come over to the house. I did not know what to do or what was going on with him. The nurse said my husband did not have long to live. I thought maybe in a few days he would leave us. My two older daughters had gone back to their homes with their families. Jayla and I were the only ones in the house with him.

The next day, he started making odd noises. He would not eat or take his medicine. I told Jayla to spend some time with her dad. I told her he was transitioning, and I didn't know how much longer he would be with us. It was September 30, 2014, and I thought we had a day or two with him.

Jayla went out to her car. When she came in the house, a sales lady selling vacuum cleaners came in with her. She wanted to show me a demonstration. I did not think it would take long, so I told her to come in. I told Jayla to go stay with her dad. Who knew it would be her last time with him?

The lady talked about the vacuum cleaner. She put a little dirt on the floor to show me how it worked. She talked for a while and I got sleepy. She called her manager to come and seal the deal.

After the manager got to the house, he came inside to the sounds of Jayla's screams. "He is gone! He's gone!" The manager and I ran in the room. He felt Jamey's neck. He said he felt a slight pulse. He was going to do CPR, but I told him not to. My husband did not want to be resuscitated.

The manager left the room. I was in the room with my daughter, trying to calm her down. She kept saying, "Bring him back!" She was laying on him and crying. I went back in the living room to see the man and lady out, but they were already gone.

I called the nurse, our pastor, and another

118

minister who helped us. Our pastor and the minister got there first. Jayla was still on her dad crying. I told her to go call her sisters and her brother and tell them their dad was gone. They all started crying on the phone. They were sad he was gone and upset they were not there to be with him. They felt bad their baby sister had to be with him alone.

The nurse came and pronounced him dead. She told me to call the funeral home to come pick him up. Tisha wanted him to stay in the house until she got there. The minister spoke to her on the phone and told her we could not wait for her to arrive. Jayla stayed on the phone crying with her sisters and brother.

I called my husband's sisters and his brother's girlfriend. The girlfriend came over to be with me. The minister told me to cry to let out my pain. I began to cry and cry. I got all of my hard crying out until I could not cry anymore because I had to be strong for my children.

The minister got Jayla out of the house. They went to the back yard. The undertakers came to

119

get my husband. When they got to the house, Jayla was screaming, "No, don't take him out of his house!"

The pastor and my brother-in-law's girlfriend went outside with me. We stood under the car porch until the undertakers were done. I saw them leave from the house with Jamey. I watched them drive away with my husband's body. I started thinking I would never see him alive again. I did not know what to do. I kept crying. It was very hot that day, so they finally convinced me to go back inside.

I started walking towards the kitchen door. I stepped up to go in the door. My legs got weak and I fell. My pastor picked me up, carried me into the house, and put me on the sofa. I felt like I could not breathe. The nurse was still in the house and told me to take it easy. She said I did not need to go to the hospital because my baby girl, Jayla needed me.

Jayla came back in the house. They told her not to worry because I was going to be alright. The nurse told me to sip a little water, take deep, slow breaths, and relax. I finally calmed down. I told my baby girl her dad was gone down the road. She said she was glad she did not see them take him because she would have been running behind the van to catch them.

It was hard for me to grasp the fact my husband was gone. His death felt surreal to me. I felt really numb. Even when he was sick, I did not feel anything. I was just going through the motions. We were together for 43 years and married for 36 years. He was the only man I'd ever known in my life. I did not cheat on him and never gave up hope the Lord would deliver him. Despite everything he put our family through, I loved him, and I did not want him to die.

My husband died on Tuesday, September 30, 2014, at around 4:30 p.m. All the children came home. The two oldest daughters said they were already planning on coming home that next day. They wished their dad could have just held on for one more day, but it was his time to go. We began to plan his funeral. I was glad to have the children there with me.

121

On Friday morning, it was time for us to go view Jamey's body. The pastor and his wife drove Darci and me. The minister and a deacon from our church went to the funeral home too. The rest of the children and Dan rode together. It was very hard for them to see him like that.

Dan called his mother's name and said something to her. Everyone stopped and looked around because he sounded just like his grandfather. We laughed about it.

I was sad, but I did not spend a lot of time at my husband's casket. He looked good laying there. Darci told the undertaker to dye his mustache because her dad did not like gray hair.

I felt empty without my husband. He was my covering and the foundation for our family. Jamey had his ways, but when he received Christ, he was there for our children and took care of his family. I had lost that covering, but I had to remind myself God was my ultimate covering. **Isaiah 54:5** says:

> *For thy Maker is thine husband...and thy Redeemer the Holy One of Israel...*

People visited us at the house from the day he died on Tuesday through Saturday. That was tiresome for my children and me. I had a friend with me all the time, but the main one I thought would be there for me was not. Yet, the one I did not expect to stand by me was there, and she was very helpful. She did whatever she could to help me. She even gave me an outfit to wear to the funeral. We scheduled the funeral for Sunday, October 5, 2014. It was a long four days from the time he died until we buried him.

God is good and He had people in place to help us. He will make a way out of no way and He will take care of you and be with you always. I thank God for one of the ministers at my church. He and his wife were very helpful to my family and me. He put my husband's suit in the cleaners and got it out when it was ready. He was even kind enough to take it to the funeral home two days before the funeral. He and his wife let me drive one of their best cars for a day. Their acts of generosity really touched me. I still pray God's blessing upon them for all the kindness they showed toward my family and me. I thank God for all my friends who were there for us. I could not have made it without them. I thank the good Lord for my church family and for their prayers as well. They also brought food to the house for us.

The night before the funeral was tough. I was so glad my sister and her two sons came down to the funeral. They stayed with us that night. My sister and I had to pray hard for the Lord to come in and take control of everything we were going through. Tisha and Jayla left for Atlanta to pick up my two grandsons who were coming to the funeral. On the day of the funeral, they made it back just before it began. I told my sister I was going to praise God at the funeral because He brought my children back in time to get ready for the funeral. God answered our prayer. I love the scripture in **Proverbs 3:5** that says:

> *Trust in the LORD with all thine heart; and lean not unto thine own understanding.*

We have to rely on God for everything. Let Him be your rock and your salvation. Put all your trust in Him. A songwriter wrote these words, he's a "Mighty Good God." I agree with that song;

124

God is good!

Jayla wanted to do a short sermon for her dad at the funeral. I told the pastor and he said she could do it before he got up to do the eulogy. The funeral was a little longer than I thought it would be. We just let the Lord have His way. We praised the Lord for a while. My two grandsons and my son made remarks. I was surprised they got up and spoke. It was a spiritual funeral. My husband would praise the Lord in church when he was living, so I did not want to have a quiet and sad funeral. We rejoiced and celebrated his life.

Jayla did a great job. Her topic was, "At This Time." I was so proud of her and I know her dad would have been proud of her too. Her scripture reference was **Ecclesiastes 3:1-4**, which says:

> *To every thing there is a season, and a time to every purpose under the heaven: A time to be born, and a time to die; a time to plant, and a time to pluck up that which is planted; A time to kill, and a time to heal; a time to break down, and a*

> *time to build up; A time to weep, and*
> *a time to laugh; a time to mourn, and*
> *a time to dance.*

It was good to see my sister and her two sons from New Jersey. My brother and his family came from Washington, DC, and my husband's brother came from California. We all had a nice visit. My husband's family was helpful to us too. Jayla went to Atlanta to visit with her sister for a little while.

When everyone went back to their own homes, I was alone, and I began to think back on things. God is so good. I thanked Him for all the help I received when Jamey was sick. He saw me through all those months of taking care of my husband without getting much rest. I thank Jesus for his promises I could hold onto in **Psalms 30:5**:

> *Weeping may endure for a night,*
> *but joy cometh in the morning.*

I needed to escape the lies and gossiping going on at home about the funeral, his suit, the casket, and other things. I needed to get away for a short time. I did not want to be a part of any gossip or

126

drama. Around the middle of October, I went to Connecticut to visit my brothers and my sister.

I stayed up there for three weeks. I enjoyed the time I spent with my family. I had a nice time with them. However, the first week there, I was sad because I missed my husband. I felt all alone. He used to travel with me and now he was gone. While I was there, I heard more gossip about my husband's funeral. I was just about to call the people and tell them a piece of my mind, but I thought about **Exodus 14:14**, where it says:

> *The LORD shall fight for you, and*
> *ye shall hold your peace.*

Chapter 10

Time to Leave North Carolina

I finished my visit and went back home to
North Carolina. I didn't have many visitors once I
got back home. Jayla came back once I returned.
Shortly after I arrived, I started hearing gossip
about my family and me again. I could not take it,
so I went on Facebook and said my peace. I just
wanted people to know how I felt. My sister-in-law
saw the post and called me to see what happened.
She wanted to know what was going on. I told her
not to worry about it because God would work it
out. I told her God will take care of me.

I called a deacon to ask for some financial
assistance with my light bill. I had no money
coming in because my husband's check stopped,
and I was not working. The deacon told me
someone saw my daughter on Facebook with
money and other things on her page. I told him I
did not believe that because she knows I don't
have any money. I got upset with him because he
acted like he did not believe me. I told him to

forget it and that the Lord will make a way somehow.

We thought we had insurance, but to the contrary, we found out there was no insurance. So the funeral director helped by allowing us to set up a payment plan. The payment was satisfied by Darci, her husband, and me. I pray God will continue to bless the funeral director for her kindness.

I called Darci to come help me pack everything because Jayla and I were moving to South Carolina with them. I could not take the gossip and drama in North Carolina anymore. That was not my home anyway. I was only there because of my husband. Now that he was gone, there was no reason for me to stay there.

My husband's brother and cousin helped me take some things out of the house while my husband was still alive. He needed a hospital bed and other things in the house. So at least I did not have to worry about those things when I got ready to move. My daughter and her family came down before Christmas to help me pack everything up.

Packing was a hard job, and it took us longer than I thought. I thank God for all the help I had. We had a lot of boxes. I gave a few things to the minister who helped my family when my husband was sick. We put some things on the side of the road to be picked up. Wayne, along with one of the ministers, packed the truck. We took everything out the house, cleaned it, and then we were ready to go. As we prepared to leave, it was getting dark and it started to rain. I started feeling a little sick. Something was going on with my left ear. I could not hear well, but I was determined to leave anyway.

We finally got on the road to leave North Carolina. Wayne was driving the truck, Darci was driving the van, and Jayla was driving her car. It rained all the way to Columbia, and I was a little scared. I prayed all the way. Jayla and I were starting a new life in South Carolina. Getting out of North Carolina was good for us.

I felt bad about the way I let Jamey treat me for most of my life. Don't let anyone have a negative impact on you or put you down. Make sure you know who you are and hold on to that.

Love God and love yourself. Most of all, know who God is and who you are in Him. Be the best you can be and always remember the promise He made in **Psalm 27:5** that says:

> *For in the time of trouble he shall hide me in his pavilion: in the secret of his tabernacle shall he hide me; he shall set me up upon a rock.*

I may have been a foolish woman in my younger days, but God was there all the time. He saw me through all of my ups and downs. I praise the Lord for giving me strength to hold on through the good and the bad times. To God be all the glory for what he has done in my life. I thank Him so much. I am so grateful I am His child.

Now, I am free and am no longer that foolish woman!

⚞ SCRIPTURE ⚟

For I know the thoughts that I think toward you, saith the LORD, thoughts of peace, and not of evil, to give you an expected end.

Jeremiah 29:11

Epilogue

The Bible says, *"The fool has said in his heart, 'There is no God'"* (Psalms 14:1; 53:1). I was never that fool, but the foolish things I did were for my great turnaround.

The intellectual usually scratches his head at the foolishness of GOD. I was indeed bewildered at the approach God took to let me fail, learn, and come to Him. I marvel at my own approach to God, in that I didn't have to cry, beg, and plead with Him to change someone else. All I needed was God to change me. I lacked the courage to ask. But in the end, I chose God, and I am thankful not to be the young foolish woman I once was.

My big takeaway is your own happiness, peace, and fulfillment only come from within you. No one person can make you happy or fulfilled. Searching for it in any other place leaves one desolate, forsaken, and unfulfilled. Love is another attribute which comes from within. One must love himself as he loves his God and other people.

The mind or outside influences preys on low self-esteem, but you have to know who you are, know who God is, and know who God is to you. God built me up and made me wise. *"If any of you lack wisdom, let him ask of God, that giveth to all men liberally, and upbraideth not; and it shall be given him"* (James 1:5). God will never criticize anyone for wanting or asking for wisdom, after all, it is the principle thing.

Care about others' feelings. Love is not selfish or vain. This was our technical fall-out. I regret we did not do this more. Communication is the key to successful living. Jamey nor I had good communications skills; we didn't know one another. A relationship is work, but both parties must agree to work on it. We didn't listen to each other nor did we see the spirit of the person inside. I was too busy looking at the way he treated me. I just should have focused on the kind way I would treat him, which was also the way I wanted to be treated.

Do not hold on to people who are not good for you. You've heard the saying, "Hurting people hurt people." This is a true saying. We thought it was about ourselves and not about each other. Marriage is a contract, an agreement, a partnership. Initially, we did not allow Jesus to be the center of our relationship. He should be the center of all relationships.

You don't have to settle for less when God can give you the best. Let go and let the Lord have His way in your life. He can help you with all your decisions. He just needs your permission.

American relationship counselor, lecturer, author, and Ph.D., John Gray wrote the book, MEN ARE FROM MARS, Women Are from Venus. Without ever reading this book, I had my own discovery that a man and a woman think and act differently. This is why opposites attract. The more people differ, the more they are the same, so adjustments to compromise is essential.

The greatest lesson learned is one cannot change another person; one can only change oneself. The optimum change comes from God. He is the only one who can do that.

Thank you for reading this account. I pray you were blessed by it. Be wise and be the best you can be.

More About the Author

Evangelist Elma P. Lomack is a child of God. She is the daughter of the late George and Charlotte Pearson. She is the youngest of nine children. She was born in Darlington, SC, and moved to Connecticut when she was in the 5th grade. Elma graduated high school in New Haven, CT.

She has been widowed for six years. She has four children, eight grandchildren, and three great-grandchildren.

Elma went to Sandhills Community College in North Carolina and graduated with an Associate's degree in 2010. She worked at Unilever Personal Care Plant for 25 years. She retired in 2020.

She gave her life to the Lord in 1979. She received

her Elder's license in North Carolina in 2003, and her Evangelist certificate in Columbia, South Carolina, in 2018. Elma is a member of The Worship Encounter Ministries in Columbia, SC.

Elma loves serving God and people. Her motto is, "If we work together, nobody has to work harder than they should." She helps by giving her time and money when she can. She has been a choir president, a mission president, a choir director, and an associate minister. She has also served on the usher board and the church aide committee.

Elma is called a virtuous woman by her children, like the woman described in **Proverbs 31**.

CPSIA information can be obtained
at www.ICGtesting.com
Printed in the USA
JSHW062132081122
32868JS00006B/84

9 780578 762012